The Dark Opens

For Alice
at Brookline,
with thanks for
your bright attention!

Miriam Levine

The Dark Opens

MIRIAM LEVINE

Autumn House
Press

PITTSBURGH

Autumn House Press Staff
Executive Editor and Founder: Michael Simms
Executive Director: Richard St. John
Community Outreach Director: Michael Wurster
Co-Director: Eva-Maria Simms
Fiction Editor: Sharon Dilworth
Special Projects Coordinator: Joshua Storey
Associate Editors: Anna Catone, Laurie Mansell Reich
Assistant Editor: Courtney Lang
Editorial Consultant: Ziggy Edwards
Media Consultant: Jan Beatty
Tech Crew Chief: Michael Milberger
Intern: Rebecca Clever
Volunteer: Jamie Phillips

ISBN: 978-1-932870-19-0

for John Lane

■   **The Autumn House Poetry Series**

Michael Simms, Executive Editor

Snow White Horses, Selected Poems 1973–88 by Ed Ochester

The Leaving, New and Selected Poems by Sue Ellen Thompson

Dirt by Jo McDougall

Fire in the Orchard by Gary Margolis

Just Once, New and Previous Poems by Samuel Hazo

The White Calf Kicks by Deborah Slicer ● 2003, selected by Naomi Shihab Nye

The Divine Salt by Peter Blair

The Dark Takes Aim by Julie Suk

Satisfied with Havoc by Jo McDougall

Half Lives by Richard Jackson

Not God After All by Gerald Stern (with drawings by Sheba Sharrow)

Dear Good Naked Morning by Ruth L. Schwartz ● 2004, selected by Alicia Ostriker

A Flight to Elsewhere by Samuel Hazo

Collected Poems by Patricia Dobler

The Autumn House Anthology of Contemporary American Poetry, edited by
Sue Ellen Thompson

Déjà Vu Diner by Leonard Gontarek

Lucky Wreck by Ada Limon ● 2005, selected by Jean Valentine

The Golden Hour by Sue Ellen Thompson

Woman in the Painting by Andrea Hollander Budy

Joyful Noise: An Anthology of American Spiritual Poetry, edited by Robert Strong

No Sweeter Fat by Nancy Pagh ● 2006, selected by Tim Seibles

Unreconstructed: Poems Selected and New by Ed Ochester

Rabbis of the Air by Philip Terman

Let It Be a Dark Roux: New and Selected Poems by Sheryl St. Germain

Dixmont by Rick Campbell

The River Is Rising by Patricia Jabbeh Wesley

The Dark Opens by Miriam Levine ● 2007, selected by Mark Doty

● winner of the annual Autumn House Press Poetry Prize

Other Books by Miriam Levine

Poetry

Friends Dreaming
To Know We Are Living
The Graves of Delawanna

Nonfiction

Devotion: A Memoir
A Guide to Writers' Homes in New England

Fiction

In Paterson: A Novel

Acknowledgments

Grateful acknowledgment to the following magazines in which some of these poems first appeared, sometimes in earlier versions:

American Poetry Review	*Mangrove*
The Boston Phoenix	*Noctiluca*
Confrontation	*Poet Lore*
The Cortland Review	*Press*
Descant	*Virginia Quarterly Review*
Harvard Review	*Women's Review of Books*
Jeopardy	*Zuzu's Petals Quarterly*

Thanks above all to Alan Feldman whose help with the manuscript made the publication of this book possible. For encouragement and help along the way, gratitude to all my poetry-reading friends, especially to Roger Freudigman, Helen Heineman, Patricia Hampl, Marilyn Harter, Betsey Houghton, Stephen Love, Julia Markus, Jim Moore, Evelyn Perry, and Phil Zuckerman.

For wonderful places to write, my appreciation to Château de Lavigny International Writers' Colony; Fundación Valparaíso; Hawthornden Castle International Retreat for Writers; Ledig House International Writers' Colony, where my stay was funded by the Diane Cleaver Fellowship; Villa Montalvo Estate for the Arts, and Yaddo.

Lines from "The Prisoner's Dream" by Eugenio Montale from *The Storm and Other Poems*, translated by Charles Wright, copyright 1978 by Oberlin College Press. Used by permission of Oberlin College Press.

Contents

Candlewood

for Julia

We go into dark and dark opens.
Boats tipped with light and moon on the water.
There is no difference between the tree and the shadow of the tree.
There is no space between light and the wave coming shoreward.
No break between the voice and the word.
There is no difference between your breath and your dear life.
There is no end of you.

With You

It had only to rain in sheets against the windows . . . .

And we were together again.

Do you remember how blue rain is?

How easy it was to give in.
How delicious to stop under a bridge,
steel shrinking, cold, shaking—but not us—

wipers still,
motor running hot.
The strawberry smell of rain.

Mist spun off black tires.
Slow trailing cars blurred to their future.

Soft door of the rain closed.
We couldn't see beyond the clearing.

Our delighted faces lifted to each other washed of secrets,
we waited like passengers on a fabulous train that would start again.

Twinning

My ruined face is my own, but my naked skin is Joe's,
and these flat hips he never lost.

My voice belongs only to me,
but not the pinky of my left hand bent from arthritis,
or my strong shoulders shaking in the first storm,

feet broad as paddles,
each toe a copy of his—

our hidden shyness, a mutual fund of tears, my wasted strength.

Those days in the vanishing perspective of a strange street when I miss him
I can rush home to take off my clothes at the long mirror.

There is skin smooth as a newborn's, conspiring soft eyefuls,

my baffled love doubled.

Staying In

I kiss the rain for washing away choices.

Why rush out to listen to another writer
when I can watch the horizon disappear?

Sun, rain, day, night—
any way—
the line between ocean and sky doesn't exist.

A white-out storm brings down birds and blows supple palms seaward.

I'll bend too.

There's enough wind to rip flags and knock
the yoke from my shoulders.

I've done enough chores to last a lifetime.
My scrubbed blouse hangs dripping from the rack,
my soaked socks slung over the rail.

An enormous palm frond floats in the flooded gutter.

I have no job except to praise.

Surfer at Wellfleet

for Helen

Where does he get
the patience to wait through the twilight, rocking
on his stomach in the break and surge,
head to the side, as if he were sleeping? It's freezing
in the afterglow when he finally rises on his one long ride home.

Invisible Kisses

I waited out the storm—
the fragrant cloud lined with violet raced west.

The rain came down like a hail of black arrows,
stained the boardwalk and dripped from the roof of the Tiki hut.

There were people my age who forget they are aging when they look at
the ocean.

And survivors with numbers tattooed on their arms, straight as a
bookkeeper's sum.
the ink indelibly blue, unlike the blessedly changing ocean.

This would be my prayer—if I prayed—
Please God, let everything keep changing.

The wind shifted and we pressed closer to each other.
There were five children clustered around their mother.

Tall as an Olympian rower, she shivered,
the damp sarong sagging at her hip.

Water ran in little rivers down her shoulders.
Two of her children were identical twins.

One looked at the ocean and did not move.
The other pressed her lips to her mother's belly—
lips like a tiny pink boat with two pointed sails.

She drew back her head and looked at the skin as if her lips would be
    printed there.
Finding nothing, she leaned forward and tried again, and again found nothing.
She tried once more but as before without much force—she was so small!

At last she forgot her mother and faced the ocean, the incoming waves
    already departing,
she and her twin on tiptoe, mirroring each other, even to the tendrils of
    wind-blown hair.

Ocean Drive

Some of us rush from our houses while it's still light
to reach the green allée and the red-lit colonnade.
We press our noses deep into the opening frangipani
and when the Latin band begins we dance to the end of the song.

We dip our children into the ocean and drink
their salty smiles while two feet away a man lies
drunk in the grass. The sun will burn him again.
His shoes are gone and his clothes have dried to his body like a shroud.

In the end we all have to lie down.
If I'm lucky you'll touch my hand and I'll remember
all the good you have done me and your beauty—
no one was more beautiful, your wet black hair, your hands full of roses.

White Candles

for Frank

Before you died, before you even knew you were dying,
we walked along a shore like this, talking little,
letting the foam dissolve around our ankles,
so this sunset I fall in step with you and drift
the way the waves come in.
In back of *us*—why not? I can make you here—the sun
sinks to liquid. The Italians you loved saw skies
like this. Yes, you say, wrapping your immaculate white
sweater around your thin shoulders as balconies of clouds,
gold-tipped, whip around us, and the gulls
face seaward, immensely patient.
Last night at the Century, white candles dripped
on our stone table, the wind-fed flames burned faster.
The instant one candle burned out, the waiter
replaced it, holding his lighter to the fresh white wick.
The waiters are sweet, their hair gathered back
in ponytails, white shirts, black pants, they look like dancers;
even the painting of the crucifixion is sweet—drops
of blood like pomegranate seeds in white caves
of split fruit. The bar is silver
with blue lights, and all the mirrors
banked with white candles, vesper lights.
Through the long dusk, through the ceiling-high open doors facing
the ocean, through the tall open windows,
the sound of waves coming in, the hush of the wind.
Once in Woodstock, snow drifts to the windows,
dazzling light without compromise, you told me
how this—to sit with friends, the table heaped—was
your favorite thing—this after all the books and work.
On the beach where I walk, a white candle burned down

to a stub, quenched, ahead another, until I pick up four
out of the cool sand. Pleasant in my hands, washed
candles, cool wax, wicks black, like lashes,
salty. Later I'll light them all with matches
I took from the Century—a small white box
with black lizard about to leap, but still, like the candle before it's lit.

John's Search

He likes to go out on cloudy afternoons
to buy little things for himself—a spool of black
thread, a tiny screw for his glasses.
He drives across town for shaving cream,
a lens cover for his camera, shoelaces.
He goes downtown to find a man
who will fix his favorite shoes
and discuss the possibility
of dyeing white shoes brown.
He haunts second-hand stores;
he likes the feel of dead men's
shirts worn thin as tissue paper.
He's still looking for a small single-bladed
knife to replace the one he lost in Italy.
He gets the shoemaker to stitch a new
buckle on an old belt broken to his waist.
He comes back at sunset
with a pack of colored pencils—
black, olive green, royal and navy,
gray, violet, forest green, red, orange,
hot pink, brown, yellow:
spokes of the wheel he turns
before he chooses one for the first stroke.
Tomorrow he will go out again
for a watchband light as the hair on his wrist,
the key transparent as glass
that could fit him for a moment to the world.

Stockholm Syndrome

When my husband was difficult, it was easy:
He'd run from my yell, and I'd know myself.

Now he's nice, an influence, so civilized.

I sit with him in the shade of the pink umbrella,
and call my mother every morning after I've read *The Times*.

When the Mexicans ascend on scaffolds to drill the balcony,
I too say, "They're here, *los de abajo*."

It makes me happy to save quarters, notice a terrier's superior gait,
remember to write the number of the check on the invoice I've just paid.

But though I've tried, I'll never lie like a soldier on a stretcher
for the whole afternoon, dying to music.

How he gives himself over, as if he's in love with Violetta.
Not that he's swooning.

How does he do it?
Half dozing, half waking, letting the notes enter him as I cannot?

To tell the truth: I can barely copy him.
His stride is too long
and he throws a huge shadow.

He can swim from blue shallows into dark water,
his kick throwing up white spume steady as a fountain.

Sitting with one hand on his ankle, I can only dangle my feet from the edge
of his bed floating us through the world while I listen for his next breath.

Post Modern

We can still have our little salon on Meridian.
The great ones come through the silver DVD.
There's a private performance of Fellini's
I Vitelloni making the most ordinary things important.

When I press the remote button the CD player flashes
Hello and the voice of the decade rushes out:
Depuis le jour où je me suis donnée, toute fleurie semble ma destinée.
Since the day I gave myself, my destiny seems all in flower.

There are pink roses sacrificed for our pleasure.
The ceiling fan on low sends a mild breeze over
Gombrich's *Little History of the World*—
"Behind every 'Once upon a time' there is always another."

Taped to the cloudy mirror Jim's poem dries and dampens with the weather—
And time at long last for the unfamiliar, intriguing scent of self-forgetfulness.
I open the balcony door to the big shot sun and our resident troop
of mourning doves in close-fitting feathers executes the end of the ballet.

My Kind of Socialism

If I remember to call out, *Buenos días, Caballero* to sullen Oscar from
    Guatemala
he stops sweeping and answers *Senora.*

His sly young-again eyes, my laugh: equal salute—for a second.

Sabrina's ready to flip out behind the post office counter
yet when I trill, "Honey, just doodads for Valentine's Day, no insurance,"
her furious face softens as her fingers hover over the little flags of the stamp

So I go about my day of no special good works.
It's so easy to feel consequential though I'm shyer than I seem.

But at the beach belonging to all of us, everyone
surrenders to a child's laugh, all of us buoyant:
naked lovers, big bellies, no one speaking or listening—
striped umbrellas a fleet of fluttering carousels.

If I shouted *Caballero, Caro, Mi Amor, Preciosa,*
I would only startle the man who gives himself
to the sun with spread legs and outflung arms;

that shivering girl—I won't make her jump—doesn't like to towel off.
Why would she, slim as lightning with the huge Atlantic dripping from
    her hair?

Strange Week

Every night there's a salty smell of burning in our rooms—
like sea water and scorched peanuts. Is someone downstairs cooking?

The noisy wind confuses us: there's not the usual sound of chairs
scraping on the floor, not one note of the song our neighbors play when
   they're eating.

Sea air salts the window glass, the metal corroded like a sunken wreck:
these windows take all my strength to open.

It's very late but no matter how tired I have to read before I can sleep,
drifting off in the middle of someone else's words, less lonely.

John falls asleep before I do. Is that really John? That man with bright
   red lips?
He's smaller, grinding his teeth, his hand scaly, his eyes slanty and weird.

I'm larger, counting my shadow and my face in the mirror.
Finally I turn off the light and we both sleep and wake up to pee.

Passing each other in the hall, we're two strangers washed in gray,
   speechless.
I blame it on the accident: 3 AM on the moon-faced clock, the motorcycle
   screaming.

John went down to see. I did not want to see. There was blood in the street,
a body twisted in the road—the man—and the girl dead in the ambulance,
   John said.

By morning, candles to San Lazaro made a little tilting fence of glass
on the hard Florida grass around the street light on the corner where
   they died.

Hurled and smashed. Days later there are rose buds cooked inside
   cellophane wrappers,
like tiny fish, sagging balloons and a picture of the dead with a card

I quote exactly: *Feliz Navidad.* "How fast you can go?
For Get your dreams. Never is sufficient. God take you because your love . . ."

The wind turns the pitiful stuff to rubbish.
The nail-head flames drowned in gritty wax.

That smell in our room smells like blood—salty and hot—and the gray of our
   night
bodies like the sooty undulations on the insides of the narrow votive
   candles.

I'd like to rip those two-by-fours from the construction site, set them on fire,
staining the sky even darker, and burn every filthy offering to the dead.

Aaron's Retreat

My uncle knew I wasn't a child
when he held out his arms to dance,
but he jerked back stiff
as if my breasts could kill.
The creases of his formal trousers grazed
my nylon-sheathed legs. My hair frosted
with his whiskey breath, our black shoes, pointed
as fox-headed stoles, his body gone,
except for cold, expert, guiding hands.
Sealed into my tight skin
I kept on going, and neither of us stumbled.
Though I was dizzy when he spun me
I knew it would pass.
His hands were as steady as when
he drove home drunk through the dark.
He could ease his silver Chrysler
up the narrow driveway, without a scratch,
though his face was white as ash, right eye
swollen closed, as if cut by the loose lace
of a boxer's glove. Ulcers burned through
thin skin along his shinbones. He held me
so far away from his ruin I thought
he was fine, both of us were,
but tonight, lost on a strange road,
when I slow down,
let every speeding car pass,
each pair of stinging headlights die,
and my oval mirror turn black
as I breathe in relief,
ahead only the beam of my own lights,
I remember how Aaron would leave the main road
and drive into the hills to dry out in a monastery.
The monks would lead him to his small cell
and he would lie down on the stiff sheet
and wait in the dark to come back to himself.

Girl at the Dance

Winter cold, cold on my bare
neck, brings it back:
a winter dance in the cavernous
Alexander Hamilton Hotel,
smoke-blackened wood,
a jumpy band, and the spinning
mirror ball throwing tiny
lit windows on the walls.

I had taken so much care with my clothes—
baby blue dress, scoop neck closed
by three rhinestone buttons,
neckline trimmed with brown fur.

A gang of boys surrounded me
but only one had the nerve to speak.
"What do you do in Passaic? What are you good at?"
"I draw," I said.
"*What* do you draw?"

I side-stepped but he ran and found a way to test me:
the yellow pencil was shorter than my thumb,
the stiff white paper curled at the edges.
"Here, show me!" He was panting like a horse.

I took them and drew birch trees glistening
in winter light because I stroked in shadows.
His face—when I snuck a look— was flushed, sharp with intelligence.
Budding connoisseur, he couldn't keep his eyes from my picture.

Hunger

Tilting the black shell,
I sucked the sack,
tongued the nub
where mussel stuck.

I tore off hunks,
sopped up sauce.
A pile of shells
wrecked on the table,
far from their rocky home.
I was ready to sail.

Ahead of me—
pink tenderloin
in a pool of juice,
brown fungi big as doorknobs
sweating on the grill.

I would learn to hold
red peppers in the flame
until the skins burned black.
Peeled, they lay tamed, musty,
half-hard on my tongue.

Tanning

In the light of noon in August
I would lie in a deck chair
on the down-slope of the yard,
my legs in yellow sun,
my head in shadow.

The sleeveless green
sheath I bought at Filene's
still lay flat between my hips
though I was pregnant I didn't show.
My arms and legs were slim,

my hair smoothed to my head,
gathered in a loop that I
pinned close with a barrette.
Even so a few strands would stray.

From time to time I would shift my legs,
letting the sun have its way.
I would lift my eyes from my book
and look down through green unfenced yards
through the willows' dragging branches.
I wanted to be all unbroken gold
before birth opened and changed me.

A car would pass. From a distance I could hear
the bark of my neighbor's chocolate Lab.
Anonymous and alone as I would not be for years,
I would run my hands over my darkening legs.

Pubescent

Palm down,
hard wrist a neck between swellings,
pores starred,
roughened skin red over knuckles,
once weak as bud-teeth
when he pressed his hand into me.

It was a soft crab I'd lift
to my mouth and nip the nail-ends.
Ripe and broken, I let him latch on,
head heavy in the crook of my arm.

Above the peak of gold hair,
a pulse beat through the plushy soft spot,
forehead rippled like a puppy's,
his brain so close under my lips
I smelled his soft new life.

He's older now and I kiss him
lightly and hardly ever touch him.
He lifts his head into light; the down on his cheek turning
silver and seeming to move as if light stroked him . . . only light.

Daughter

You beg for a tattoo like your friend's.
A band of stars at your ankle.
There's no way to escape regret.
Indelible dye makes it worse.

Growth spurts knock you out.
The cold makes you drowsy.
That's nothing new.

Don't sleep too long.
Dark night never gets tired of holding you.

Get up and remember the song.

You can sing as you dart and kick:
I have to be careful when I dance.
My dye-job is fading.
And white hair grows at the roots.

What do you want me to do? Lie here with you?

Or break every mirror and never go out?
I'll wait for the sun to light us both.

You're on your feet. We're facing the same way,
the sun does what it's supposed to do,
the mirror angled to the window,
your face just behind mine.

Girl on the Subway

Her blouse is made of transparent linen
with cloudy white flowers across the shoulders.

The ends—just a few—of her long blond hair
cut to form a point at her waist like a shawl

swing back and catch on the knee of the man
directly in back of her on the aisle.

He can't feel them through denim jeans and doesn't see
the gorgeous spider-silk shine—
we've all had such losses and not even noticed.

Surprise

Steam from the shower clouds the mirror
except for the lower left corner above the lit candle.

The dry corner, blue as ice and shaped like a flame,
reflects my hip and the smoky taupe tile.

There's even a bit of my hand and a piece of the shower curtain
called "Disco," which has silver facets stamped in the plastic.

I'm leaving my wet body to live on the other side of the mirror—
like looking in through a hole in the second-floor window.

Where am I standing? On a ladder?
Who is that dripping and coated with steam?

She's staring—amazed.
What is she staring at?

That dry bit of mirror,
the shape of a flame.

Alpine Strawberries in November

What's the matter with me?
I'm supposed to know about words.
I told people the name of these berries

without paying attention to what I was saying.
I would pick them in the sun and eat them warm.
Not like this, and never in the cold.

They smell like mountains,
strange new love,
thin air hard to breathe.

I'm kneeling on cold flagstones.
My gloves are off.
There's frost;

the clouds are black, the wind from the north.
My chapped lip splits, my knees are freezing,
but I've got a whole delicious handful,

wine-sweet, but with a sting,
a taste like flint and snow,
eau-de-vie, icy red and soft.

Another One

When I bend and stroke
the young Airedale
she jumps to my touch,
the damp of her beard
and the deep curl
of black and tan fur
against my hands
like the feel of Daisy.

Like Daisy: cunning
light in her eyes,
prance and bump,
rough black
nose with nostril
slits like hieroglyphs.
Yip and lick
of rough pink tongue.

Press closer, darling, go ahead, shift your stocky shoulders against my knees
the way Daisy used to, trusting, sure of love, that glint always in her
    topaz eyes.
That's it—paw on my foot—weight, sharp nails' skid; tickle,

I can take it—subtle—

through my shoe.

At the Piroska Café

—Sipping coffee at the table near the window.
—Music I can't identify.
—A woman writing in a black and gold notebook.
—A man reading.
—Taste of coffee made as I want it.
—Buttery croissant.
Sublunary pleasures I love!

An old woman comes in with a child.
"Nana, let's sit *here*, there are flowers."
Freesias are in, budded stems opening yellow at the tips.
The child lifts a little green box of Crayolas,
slips out red with an arcing hand and bends
so close her hair drifts on the paper.

A woman leans back and lights a cigarette,
frizzed-out black hair against the white wall.
The door opens and closes, the sound
of the street fades in and out like the voices around me.
Through the glass a bare linden.

Copying her grandmother's gestures
as if she were looking in a mirror
the child puts on her own hat,
a man takes off his glasses and lets the room blur.
The fragile loose-woven day, the patient
order of afternoons, returns and returns.
Surely that linden will open its white porches where I dream,
so why am I grieving?
Why do I write in my notebook,
"Don't take this away"?

Art Class

None of us is any good at getting a likeness except our teacher
whose work is technically perfect and lifeless.

I'm better at noticing how we gasp as we draw—one of us moans—
the rubbing rasp of boot soles on the concrete floor,

wet brushes where the colors mass ready to become . . .

"Which artist do you love? Copy him!" our teacher says.
Copy? I'm an intimate of Van Gogh: unconsummated love.

At the Met I saw his painting of two sunflowers,
just the blossoms, like vegetables laid on a chopping board.
He must have cut the stems. They're too tough to break, unlike bones.

The flower that faces us is a huge complex eye,
the other's glory hidden beyond the stub and scalloped butt.

I bet he painted the backside so he could get that green.

The color under the black skin of an avocado is a little like it—
the night-time green of baseball fields— but his glows more, an unearthly hu

He must have surrendered, as if the flowers were Vincent
and he had metamorphosed into curves of green and they into him.

Still he could bring his power to every stroke—while I lose mine.

Seeing his sunflowers side by side, I felt a tearing in my chest,
appreciation raw and defeated, my little life swooned away.

Happiness

for L.L.

There are tiny tables on open balconies,
a pink phone near a chair, the ocean waving its enormous blue flag.

If you came with me you'd hear wind sputter in the umbrella fringe,
lungs open, bad heart forgotten.

A lonely orphan famished for a kiss, the artist Aaron Rose
found he loved the milky skin of Chinese vases at the Met:
"I saw the great pieces weren't filled with misery, they were filled with life."

Cup on the table, dog leaping to the ball,
each body, each face, ocean edge, wave crest: the same.
"Light is going around everything"—if only we'd see.

After Disappointment

It's a relief to lean against the wall and watch lilies
with their stamens tipped with tiny moons dropping pollen.
Do the dressy petals feel it as balm? I do—and that smell like rain.

It helps to rename things: my troubles fading blossoms.
I'll even call my grandson's face a lily. I'll say the bruise
from his fall is pink as a lily and the abrasion curved like a petal.

I'll say the letter that came today is "food for a poem."
Rolling it like a cigarette, taking care not to hurt myself,
I'll put a match to the twisted bit of paper and burn every word.

On the Way to Katie & Dave's

The first rest stop in New Hampshire on Route 93
is big enough for an Indian wedding,
the groom riding in on a white horse, the whole village invited.

There's a wood fire burning in a six–foot high hearth.
The burning logs are orange and at the center where the flame is hottest
the grain shows like the flakes that show in fish as it cooks.

Standing next to me in front of this great fire you would know
if you looked at me how much you were shining.

Minutes of the Poetry Group,
Robert's House, West Canton Street

for L. who was absent

When you called to say you couldn't make it,
I was standing in the red room looking out,
white lights of perpetual Christmas on the balcony.
City heat had melted the snow and the yard was green.
In back of me, Robert's friendly understanding voice—
what are we if not understanding? You've moved
to Jason Courts, "not even a calendar pinned up"
where you can see it—your white lie—
"not a plate unpacked, not a piece of fruit."
I wish you would leave your unhappy life
and come to us who will feed you as
your drunken husband never can.
Waist-high under Robert's fingers:
salsa, black bread in little squares,
wheat crackers, five cheeses, one striped gold and white,
tulip glasses filled with purple-black port;
on a marble slab, smoked salmon,
the delicate muscle destroyed for us.
The fire burned, the loud bell jangled—Alan.
The front hall is small as a French elevator:
"Isn't this foreign?" I began. And with a patient smile
Alan listened. The steep stairs fell behind him.
How large we were in our smallness. I read a poem
in imitation of Alan's loving letters, but where he
would write to the living, I wrote to the dead.
Robert gave us Montale: *I am no different than the moth wings*
my shoes keep powdering to dust on the tiles,
than the iridescent kimono of light . . .
No matter how perfect the great ones,
their metaphors drilling doors between rooms
that don't seem to exist in the same world,
we went on with our poems as you would,

so Alan took his turn: *But words*
need to be aimed at someone's
need to listen. Like electrical current
which doesn't actually travel
when it leaps between two charges.
I want you to need to listen
as you need to breathe—
what a boss I am.
Forgive me: it's better here.
Robert's canary—have you seen
it high in the hot corner, orange as mango?—
trilled its lushness, the salmon on my tongue.
"Is *that* an ordinary canary?" Alan asked.
A log crashed out of the fire, and the smaller flaming
pieces settled with a low undersong.

"Oh, yes, ordinary. They told me to feed it paprika
to keep it orange, but I don't
and it hasn't lost its color.
Someone across the yard has one.
When it's warm, we put the cages out. They sing
across the garden—the males sing." We missed you.

In the Magnifying Glass

In Atget's photos some people dissolve in long exposures.
A white blur tells me someone was there, someone moved and disappeared
But under my magnifying glass I can make out a wisp of a girl,
dress like a crumpled flower, a face in the hedge, a dog at loving attention.

The streets glisten with rain, white sky above the filthy
scarred buildings: clouds are always moving.
There's a boy at a window, looking down from the dark
triangle made by the drape caught on his shoulder,
his face grave as a hero's on a coin.

None makes an impression on the severe beauty of the streets—
not the man with alert ardent eyes or the woman whose white dress
skirts the damp road, clasped hands like two tiny lockets.
White flames of the sycamore leaves. Blazing white stairs.

Mother

The watch you give me is thin as a dime,
crimped at the edges with platinum
set with diamonds; its tiny hands tremble
like a needle on a compass—a fortune!

I want to pay but you won't allow it.
You're at the register, ringing up the sale.
Each number actually rings, the zeros, too,
the total like a merry-go-round tune.

The drawer shooting out makes the counter shudder.
You put your money in the right compartments
and push in the drawer which has raised corners
like the corners to hold photos in an album.

I wonder if you own this grand store.
We never had much money but now you wear a fur coat
smelling of fresh snow and lilac so the air is tinged with lilac—
the color—and we see each other more clearly.

"I love to be surrounded by people," you say.
And you did, but only in the afternoon, choosing the best listener.
I've seen you lean toward that one, your beautiful mouth
shaping your words like kisses, secret kisses.

It's three o'clock when work is done and dinner won't be ready for hours.
I'll wait with you under the elephant-foot beech and never look at my watch
though the needle-hands advance like years. You taught me to tell time.
Darling, there's so much time to squander. Why are you suddenly quiet?

Saturday Morning

Maybe it's because I can do anything
I want in my sleep that when I get up
I feel like a fish the ice fisherman
dumped on the snow-coated ice.
But in a few minutes the kettle is steaming.
My little Florida, I say as I cup my cup, and drink up heat.
I write my yellow checks with a blue pen
full of green ink; I put letters into blue envelopes
and press on thin stamps like delicate flags.
There is always somewhere to go in the endless work
of taking care of ourselves—Post Office, Bank, Dry Cleaner.
I'm on my way to the dressmaker to fix
the black slacks I bought last summer and left on a chair
I passed every morning on my way to work
and stopped noticing, like a dying un-watered plant.
There's a Russian New Year's Eve tree at Anna's,
the frosted glass balls floating
from green branches, Mozart on the radio.
Anna makes me stand in the small white circle
as she kneels and pins. *My English still so poor.*
Friends bring me this book. She holds up Malamud's "New Life."
I love him. I read him in Russian, different title.
Last time she asked me if I were Jewish.
She could tell by my name. *Mariam,* she pronounced it.
Me also, she said across the shining cones of thread.
Her blunt-cut, red-gold hair swings across her cheeks;
her teeth are the color of pinkish-white coral.
She glides to the counter; her fish-skin wool skirt
sheathes her legs without a wrinkle,
like wet skin slipping across fat and bone,
flaring gray-black just below her knees.
Pick up next week, my mermaid murmurs.

Knowing

after Simone Martini's
"Annunciation to the Virgin"

Mary's hand is hooked like a claw at the neck of her dress,
the sleeve edged with red, a red book in one hand—the bible is so full of blood.

She turns her back on the angel. Our Lady of Fury and Sorrow.
Only a monster wants to see her son nailed to a cross.

Even the lily in a pot on the floor knows the future, its black stem bristling
   with thorns.
So much gold, the angel all in gold, like a Christmas ornament.

That fabulous branch in the angel's hand—she won't touch it.
She knows the future because the painter looking back through time makes
   her know.

We know, too, in a general way, how life will end, and before the end: sorrow
   and pain.
Is our sorrow less than hers? I don't know. If we see angels, they lock us up.

Most of us don't see them. In spite of what we know we still don't turn away.
In our ordinary lives we usually take a flower. "It's gorgeous," we'll say—

or something like that—and forget the flower is dying, as we are.

Glads

"Fading"? Open your eyes! I live with them.
These tips plump like pink cigars
while spent ones close their used mouths,

soft clotted knots: wet, cooked berries,
catch of scorched jam at the bottom of the pot.
That's the color: burnt cherry, fire, blood.

You *still* don't see it?
Try this!
The shriveling blossoms are curled feet
streaked with purple-red henna.

And the bride whose feet are painted
gives birth to a child.
His face doesn't brighten—not yet.

It darkens

with her blood.

Singe: Beauty Ritual

When I open Jen's lipstick, slide the slippery
grease over my lips—mouth full of melting violet—
I see her lean toward the burner shooting blue flame.
Watch, she whispers; and rocks her arms through the blue roar,
scorch smell of singed hair, like the burn
in the live chicken market—blood in the sawdust.
Feel, she commands, stretching her hairless rippling arms
toward my hands that tremble over her living unbroken skin.

Red Bud

Except for earrings red bud is naked.
Weather licks her shaking arms.

Redder and redder red bud
pushes out flowers,
drops pollen on the wind.

Fresh fans open and flirt,
darker green as they age, crimson as they fall;
red bud undresses in the rain,

jewels in the jewel box, sap sinking;
underground, roots mingled with worms,
sucking up water under the snow.

Stripped like a New Year's Day swimmer, red bud stays to drink.

Nor, Seven-Months Pregnant

She carries high,
belly pushing up small
pointy tits; everywhere else
she's thin as a cat,
delicate, farouche.
Piss-off yellow eyes.

She hasn't turned the light on.
At the end of August, her
room is dusky, the window
where she stands, gold
and green as an orchard.
She's fastening big button
earrings, fake mother-
of-pearl; frosted glass bangles,
pale green and smoke, hang
like ice from her throat. Wild
with cabbage roses, her sweater
comes down to her crotch,
thighs gloved in back pinstripe.

"Let's go," she says, and stops.
The light behind her head
lights up her gold bob,
fine fuzz on her slender neck.
The mouth is dark now,
close to the teeth.
Nor is staring, stunned
anger in her eyes.
Her tough hands rest
for a second on the high
curve of her belly.
One foot is forward. Across
the inside ankle-bone: a spill
of broken running stitches—complex—
a blue so dark it makes the paler veins look childish.

Peg's Story

He came out looking old,
a deep, slanting fold
under each sealed eye.
The good Irish nurse
showed me how to hold
him. Long back pressed
against my inner arm,
the weight of his head
filled my hand, his neck
on the thick flat of my
wrist. Tucked in the elbow
crack, the cool unmarked
feet, solid as soap.

For two days he sucked
weakly and slept, thumb-
end of a heart against my
heart. On the third day, he
howled, he sucked so hard,
I had to break the suction
with my finger to shift
him to the other side.
Strange new food flowed
over his clean tongue. He
called the milk out of me.
I was always good in
the dark. But one hot
day—the first of summer—
I let him cry too long
and found him pushing up
on the backs of his hands.
He had worked himself
up to the headboard,

poor fingers rubbed
raw across the knuckles.
I hope you don't mind
listening. I wince too.
Still, a good thing: forgiveness.
And forgetting? Just as good.

Breather

I can't remember your first word
but feel—
hot drowse,
those mornings:
kettle steaming,
window full of light,
room half-dark.
So far away only near-
sighted texture of things
comes back.

Your cry—
I heard you
from downstairs,
through walls.
My lullaby:
Dave, sleep,
Snow sticks,
Wind blows,
Tree shakes.

I rocked you running a fever, sucking until eyes crossed,
lids I saw blink—slow, slower:

easy swoon, sleep.

Your let-go.
My tuck-in.

I had enough energy to push through snow-shagged hemlocks—and breath

Now I'm watching words form on my laptop's blue screen.

You?
You're flying on skies.

Fight

I grabbed Dave's shoulders.
He slid in my grip, skin
hard as bone. The sound
of my yell stopped him.
Blood flushed up through
his neck and face as if strong
light were turned on him.

He stood dead still,
bare chest, hard breasts,
waist a lace of muscle.
His shorts were pulled down
below his navel where my blood
once pumped into him,
legs hairy as a satyr's.

"I won't let go," I spit. "No,
No," he yelled. He hunched
his shoulders against my wild hands.
"It's late. It's night. You can't." I slapped. I ran.
I shot the bolt. "I'll lock you in. For good,"
I roared, but when I spun back, I saw
he had slipped through another door without a sound.

Return-to-Sender,
Rain-Spotted Letter I Hang Onto

Stamp stuck crooked, stuck firm, too late to change—
harmless teeth of the stamp,
flattened rose.
Name furred in black ballpoint.
Address in blue ink written days later.
Dense hedge of wrong zip scratched out in black.
My name in the left corner—
points of the peaks,
little flourish of the toes almost invisible.
Young number of my house.
Sound of my street, a wall of red brick.
Blue smudged lightning from the poles of *d*'s and *t*'s.
Shoots of arrow-wood, slanting *I*'s in the wind,
clear water whipped off branches.
Name of town a growl.
This fucking envelope. And also I was crying.

Patience

Weeks without a win.
The queens are trapped under deuces.
I could cheat: shuffle mid-game,
break out smothered cards.

Thieves just pull a gun.
Give me the money, they say,
or I'll blow out your brains.
They call it winning.

Me? I'll lay out the cards again.
In time, red queen will marry black king,
each card will go home to its ace:
diamond, club, heart, spade.

We can't stand to be inside anymore
when dust rises under the maples
and a frill of ice melts in the crocus.
We go down to the broken magnolia
in the March wind that cuts through sunlight.
A slab of old snow fills the gutter
like yellow fat stuck with sawdust
in the alley behind the butcher shop.
We go on, shivering, up past the empty playground
in back of Hemenway, so dark in the blue shade against the hill
it could be moonlight, the little red benches empty and still.
At the crest of the hill the wind stops and we stop and sway,
our arms close to our sides as we try to write what we see.
The pointed shadow of my pencil on the blue-
lined card that bends under my hands.
On the arc of the hill a man and a woman play
catch, the lines of their black profiles drawn against the sun,
the arc of the ball follows the arc of the hill
to the jagged mass of the shag-bark maple—I understand
the French who lop and twist and straighten their trees, who cut
fruit trees so their carved branches flatten against a wall
so the teardrop pears swell and blush, who bandage the trunks
of lindens into white whips, who cauterize with pitch,
who straighten the teeth of the rose. Why should they have
to see a wild maple like this crack open, the giant
lateral branches shoot from the black wound and the branches
throw out suckers and the suckers crack the live branch?

Snapper

In the corner of my eye,
in the dry road,
black as a truffle,
a three-inch turtle
stamped like leather on an old book.
I take a leaf by the stem,
brush the tiny head tip.
A claw shakes.
A sequin eye opens.
It's alive!
The tail arches.
Is it fear?
From the pinpoint anus
a clear drop of liquid pearls like semen.

Back to the pond, fingers curled as if prying
open a locket, I hold the shell by the rim
so nothing touches my palm.
Down in the mud, clear of tangled weeds,
its flattened embryonic feet touch water and move.
It could live longer than I will,
a huge, domed platter, tarnished black,
leathery shoe of its head opening,
spiny teeth sharp.

Let it!

Hill's Pond

for Sarita

Just as I lie back, two red dragonflies
loop together on the rough sleeve of my sweater—
under blue-gray wings, soft amulet,
raised dots, downy and dark.

Flushed with joy, I turn to you,
but your eyes are dulled with pain—
your bones are turning to powder
and your hands won't work.

These reds promise you nothing.
Why should you be glad for me?
I'm swelling with good health
like your young Peace Rose
with its iridescent frills of light.

If I were cruel, I'd hold up this eaten leaf,
its stiff skeleton showing through white mould.
I'd say I'm thinking of *The Nature of Things*,
but it can't console you, that ancient book in Latin.

I won't tell you how beautiful and inevitable this little death is,
the lovely delicate white powder tracing the leaf ribs, the leaf
stuck with shining galls, all of its soft parts given over—
as you will be given, you and I, but first you.

Cannibal

When I see our dog plow the dead
squirrel from the dump of pine needles
and roll over the flattened carcass,
flying bits of squirrel fur stuck to her back,
I think that's what I'd like to do to you
if you died before I did. First put you out
in the weather until you shrunk
and dried like a smoked side of beef.
I would roll over your stiff body—licking, nipping,
getting your smell on me as I've done
for all of our life together. But this
time I would get under your hair,
under your skin. I would crack your bones between my jaws.
The rusty marrow would turn to liquid in my mouth, and finally I would let go.

Love

If John had said, "Love you, I miss you," I would have answered,
"Love you, miss you, too," and not especially loved him or missed him,
but when he said his friend was dead, Frankie, Frances Parker Wood—
"We were so close; we were kids together, before adolescence and all that"-
his voice caught in his throat and I loved him.

"I can't take care of anyone, I'm no Miss Nursie," my friend Susan
would tell me and I made sure to seem healthy and cheerful until eventually
worn out by my efforts I stopped loving her. But what did she know?
Every day of this long wet summer she takes care of her dying friend Owen
and will take care of him until he is dead and think of him tenderly as I now
    think of her.

Yet I'll never be as good as *Jenufa* in her opera. Before the river runs
loose in spring, when ice turns transparent, her drowned baby is found
floating under the icy lens and Jenufa melts with forgiveness though the kill
is her foster mother—*Oh Mother—under the ice!* she sings, as she feels
the killer's terrible suffering and lifts her from her knees.

Before Leaving

I cut a bunch of black-eyed susans and put them near the door
so they will be the first thing I see when I come back.

Only one night away and already I'm missing my place.

I don't have to do anything about the cicadas hissing like rain
or the throb of the mourning doves.

The wind will be here turning the poplars to silver.
The rain will have come and gone

and these flowers will be on all night
like the lamp of my insomniac neighbor;

open-eyed, sleepless, they will keep staring at me
as I walk through the door and put down my keys.

Reunion

It is a shock to hear wind rattle the door,
after such a still day, a shock to feel
cold air pour into the narrow room.
The draft bends the candle flame
and peels away smoke in one long curl.
There is a single tulip in a vase,
the only one to come back this year,
stamens like burnt wicks and silky petals
curling back and back until they have to drop,
careless of themselves as I used to be.

It is wonderful after all this time
to watch you as you seem to listen
to our friends when their talk runs ahead.
And you are thinking your own secret thoughts.
The wind picks up again—you feel it, too—
and open your lips to get more of it,
your eyes, gold-flecked and slanted,
tawny irises ringed with amber,
wing-shaped shadows at the corners
and deeper in, a weary glamour.

It is a shock clearing your place after you've left
to find my hand resting where you touched—here and here,
marking time slowly on the table, on the arm of your chair—
to feel you are still in me, as red in the flower.

The End of Spring

Look at that Daphne buttoned into her coat of leaves,
nothing but leaves—a thousand uniforms edged with white.

If I hadn't seen it, I would never believe
it could come back loaded with blossoms.

I would never believe I could walk out the front door
into the fragrance of honey and fire.

It's only a room with the ceiling blown off, I'll say.
It's only the scent of Daphne like the memory of love: everything soaked in it.

He got it right, the proportions—
I mean—of the world and our place in it.

Our place is as small as the women dancing
in each other's arms near the ocean.

Their bodies seem hardly to exist,
their feet narrow as candles,
their dresses gauzy as mist,
but we pay attention to them
and the ocean big as a mountain.

Just over their shoulders a long black wake
solid as stone streams to the vanishing point
where they could vanish if they just stepped
onto the ocean heavy as silver and smeared
with moonlight thick as triple crème, bad for us and so delicious

they say it could kill us. That ocean could. Endlessly black, nearly
    endlessly deep.

Footstep

I heard my footstep, nothing else.
My horizon was a hat brim!

A sob swelled in my chest.
I couldn't catch my breath.

Is this all there is?

As if to answer, the wind ripped off my hat.

Shadows fell from the maples.

There was the pond, there was the sky.

The morning ghost of a moon.
A flood of clouds.

The wind moaned.

Give me a minute of silence
so I can listen for my footstep.

Give me back my hat and the shadow like twilight.

More, more, more, the wind sang.
The obedient sparrows covered the grass.

And the grass delivered the earth as a booming finale.

Reflection

The pond must be still—or nearly still—
to produce these wonderful reflections.
The few angry notes of one o'clock
do not matter. The pond does not
hear the sputter of the power motor,
the idiot yelling, "Son of a bitch,
I said *Heel*." The pond does not care.

If the air is still, if there's enough light,
the pond reflects whatever is near,
and far—the blue curving sky, and those gulls.
I seldom come here at night—not even
when the moon is out and the water trembles.
A muddy smell rises like regret and that trembling,
no matter how enchanting, reminds me of weeping.

Night Walk: Winter Solstice

Night says, *Touch my face I'll make you dark, unending.*
I feel touched. By what? The dark has no shape.
I touch rough bark and lean against the leaning tree to gain a footing and
    go on.
John's already reached the pond where once he saw a boy fall thru the ice
    and drown.

The shaggy pines, dark on dark, lean toward the water, too.
It's terrible to be rooted forever like Daphne, I think,
unable to smell her own luscious scent or see her hands or feel her heart,
forever to breathe as trees breathe through their leaves.

"Are you thinking of turtles, under water?" John asks as if we're one person.
"Do they hibernate like bears? Bears give birth in hibernation;
their hearts don't seem to beat; half dead, they hardly breathe. But they nurse.
The cubs, the size of thumbs at first, come out fat and glossy in the spring."

Someone in the house above the pond turns on a light.
An icy wake flashes across the pond as if the house
were moving through the night. The light goes out.
The house *is* moving, everything sailing through the dark.

I do not want to sleep or eat or think of spring.
I want only to keep on walking with John thru the dark world.
It's easier now we're on soft loam and leaf mold; the soles of my shoes
    suddenly thin,
I feel the dirt yield. Thin and transparent—I'm seeing through my feet:
    earth, brown leaf.

If we go on we might force the night to bloom in us like narcissus
put down early in the dark, stony hard, to send out their white scented stars.

Notes

"Stockholm Syndrome," a state in which the captive adopts the style of the captor. The phrase *los de abajo* means "those from below." Violetta is the leading soprano role in Giuseppe Verdi's *La Traviata*.

"Post Modern." *Depuis le jour où me suis donnée, toute fleurie semble ma destinée*, Gustave Charpentier, *Louise*. "And time at long last for the unfamiliar, intriguing scent of self-forgetfulness," Jim Moore, "Blood Harmony," *Lightning at Dinner*, Graywolf Press, 2005, page 26.

"In the Magnifying Glass." Eugène Atget (1856–1927).

"Mother." In memory of Gertrude Levine, 1908–2004.

"Singe: Beauty Ritual." In memory of my aunt, Jennie Levine, 1897–1985.

"Happiness." The words of the photographer Aaron Rose are quoted in *Aaron Rose: Photographs* by Alfred Corn, Harry N. Abrams, 2001.

"Minutes of the Poetry Group, Robert's House, West Canton Street." "I am no different than the moth wings/ my shoes keep powdering to dust on the tiles,/ than the iridescent kimono of light . . . . " Eugene Montale, "The Prisoner's Dream," *The Storm & Other Poems*, translated by Charles Wright, Field Translation Series I, 1978, page 136.

"Love" refers to the opera *Jenufa* by Leos Janácek (1854–1928).

Design and Production

Cover and text design by Kathy Boykowycz
Cover painting, *Orange Sky*, by Nancy Clark

Text and titles set in Boton, designed by Albert Boton, 1986

Printed by Thomson-Shore of Dexter, Michigan,
on Nature's Natural, a 50% recycled paper